A FREE GIFT FOR YOU!

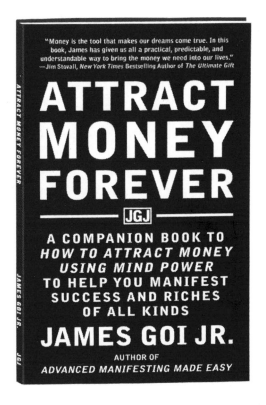

Attract Money Forever will deepen your understanding of metaphysics and mind-power principles as they relate to attracting money, manifesting abundance, and governing material reality. You'll learn how to use time-tested, time-honored, practical, and spiritual techniques to be more prosperous and improve your life in astounding and meaningful ways. Visit jamesgoijr.com/subscriber-page.html for your free download copy of this amazing book and to receive James' free monthly *Mind Power & Money Ezine*.

HOW TO ATTRACT MONEY USING MIND POWER

Books by James Goi Jr.

How to Attract Money Using Mind Power

Attract Money Forever

Ten Metaphysical Secrets of Manifesting Money

Also

Advanced Manifesting Made Easy

Aware Power Functioning

The God Function

And

My Song Lyrics (multiple volumes)

JGJ Thoughts (multiple volumes)

<u>Note</u>

James continues to write new books. To see
a complete list, visit James on Amazon at
Amazon.com/author/JamesGoiJr

HOW TO ATTRACT MONEY USING MIND POWER

JGJ

A CONCISE GUIDE TO MANIFESTING ABUNDANCE, PROSPERITY, FINANCIAL SUCCESS, WEALTH, AND WELL-BEING

JAMES GOI JR.

JGJ

JAMES GOI JR.
LA MESA, CALIFORNIA

ISBN:
978-1-68347-000-7 (Trade Paperback)
978-1-68347-001-4 (.mobi)

Published by:
James Goi Jr.
P.O. Box 563
La Mesa, CA, 91944
www.jamesgoijr.com

"The writer does the most who gives his reader the most knowledge and takes from him the least time."

—Sydney Smith

"Order and simplification are the first steps toward the mastery of a subject …"

—Thomas Mann

CONTENTS

PREFACE

If you had all the money you wanted, what would you do? Where would you live? How would you spend your time? Are you willing to change the way you think so you *can* have all the money you want? In this book, you will learn how to do just that.

This system for attracting money works like magic. But it's *not* magic. It's based on sound metaphysical laws. There have always been a select few who have known these laws. Today, more people than ever before are learning and using these once closely-held secrets of attraction and manifestation.

This book boils down the basics taught by many other writers. And it quotes 160 of those writers. The quotes carry information *and energy*—the energy of those writers *and* of all the teachers and writers who affected them.

This book will affect *you*. You will never view money or your mind the same. Practice what you learn here, and your struggle for money will be over. You will attain all the money you want using a simple process of cause and effect.

This book will change you. It will enlighten you. It will show you how to live the full, prosperous, creative life you have always wanted to live. That new life can begin right now.

Big promises, yes. This little book delivers on them. It was written for every person who has ever yearned to have more, to give more, to be more. This book was written for you.

Turn the page. And never look back. Your dreams of an unlimited, never-ending flow of all the money you could ever use are about to turn into reality.

1

DESIRE

Desire is the great moving power of the mind—that which excites into action the will and powers of the individual. It is at the bottom of action, emotion or expression.

—Robert Collier
The Secret of the Ages, 1926

CONCEPTS AND COUNSEL

Desire is the feeling of wanting something. It is the emotion that prompts all human action. To cause yourself to act on your desire for more money, *increase* your desire for more money.

Emotion is power. So, the stronger you can make your emotion of desire for money, the more power you'll have to *get* money. The more money you want, the more desire you'll need to build.

Your desire for more money has caused you to act by picking up this book. You are now moving forward. Desire breeds action. That action then feeds the desire. That increased desire then breeds even more action. Once you push yourself to get the process going, the process will tend to pull you in and pull you along.

You are now in the process of getting all the money you want. Keep reading this book. Think as this book instructs you to think. Act as this book instructs you to act. In these ways, you will strengthen your desire for more money. In these ways, you will propel yourself down a sure path to more money.

This *sure* path to more money is also a *narrow* path. If you desire too many things at once, you will wander aimlessly. You will advance slowly, if at all. To get the money you want, you'll have to focus your mind and your efforts. Be willing to delay starting other projects that you can let wait awhile.

Build up your desire for the money you want and set lesser desires aside. Do this, and you'll have all the power you need to get your money. In the pages to follow, you'll learn to *wield* that power in a way that will ensure you get what you're after.

SIMPLE STEPS

1. At the top of a clean sheet of paper, write THINGS I'VE WANTED TO DO. List activities such as *learn to play guitar* and *remodel the basement*. List from five to twenty or more items.

2. Go through the list and cross off any items that can wait until *after* you're well on your way to getting the money you want. The fewer items on your final list, the better. You can leave an item, say a hobby you want to take up, if it will help you relax and take your mind off your work from time to time.

3. Number the remaining items in the order you want to do them. Rewrite them under THINGS TO DO. Do something *today* toward getting the first item done. Keep referring back to the list, at least weekly, and do what's needed to complete the tasks.

4. Use the time and energy you would have used on the crossed-off items to do what you need to do to get the money you want.

5. Title your next list WHY I WANT MORE MONEY. List reasons such as *work less/more free time* and *new kitchen for Mom*. List all the reasons you can think of. Try for at least ten.

6. Read that list at least monthly to remind yourself *why* you want more money. This will help keep your desire alive and growing. Add new items you think of and delete items you've accomplished.

WHAT OTHERS HAVE WRITTEN

Desire is. the creator; but when desire is spread
over a host of things it … accomplishes little.
—Elizabeth Towne, *How to Grow Success,*
1904

Preceding accomplishment must be desire.
Thy desires must be strong and definite.
—George S. Clayson, *The Richest Man in Babylon,*
1926

Desire is at the bottom of every achievement.
—Orison Swett Marden, *How to Get What You Want,*
1917

Desire creates the power; power inspires the mind of
the individual, and success is the result of
that inspiration rightly applied.
—Raymond Holliwell, *Working with the Law,*
1964

… Men draw toward themselves that
which they Desire.—William Walker Atkinson,
Dynamic Thought, 1906

Remember that desire is the first law of gain.
—James K. Van Fleet, *Hidden Power,*
1987

Whatever may be the scale on which we exercise
our creative ability, the motive power
must always be desire.
—Thomas Troward, *The Hidden Power,*
1921

2

BELIEF

Belief changes the tempo of the mind or thought-frequency. Like a huge magnet, it draws the subconscious forces into play, changing your whole aura and affecting everything about you— including people and objects at great distances.

—Claude M. Bristol
The Magic of Believing, 1948

CONCEPTS AND COUNSEL

Belief is the acceptance of a notion as being true. Your beliefs regarding money govern how much money you get. Beliefs naturally evolve over time. And they can be purposely changed by design.

With some thought, you know what your conscious money beliefs are. You should develop those that help bring money to you. You should discard those that keep money from you. You often do *not* know what your *subconscious* money beliefs are, but you can get around that fact—this book will teach you how to form new subconscious beliefs that will displace and void old subconscious beliefs.

Managing your subconscious beliefs is a crucial step in using mind power to attract money. Your subconscious mind—or simply, "subconscious"—attracts and repels money all the time. It does this with or without your conscious knowledge or consent.

Your subconscious is sheer creative power devoid of will and judgment. It cannot tell which of your mental impressions are of real things, and which are of imagined things. It believes *all* mental impressions represent real objects and situations.

Your subconscious doesn't know if mental impressions are of things helpful or harmful, wanted or unwanted. It just does all in its power to bring about what it is led to believe exists. And your subconscious has *vast* power. It affects your and other people's thoughts, feelings, and actions. Too, it affects circumstances directly—*without* the help of human action.

Create and cultivate the belief that you have all the money you want, and your subconscious mind will make it a reality.

SIMPLE STEPS

1. To help build and maintain the conscious and sub-conscious beliefs you need to attract money, read from this book daily.

2. Under MY MONEY BELIEFS, list those conscious beliefs you can think of: *it takes money to make money; money is hard to come by; money always seems to show up when I really need it.*

3. Next to each listed belief, put a *G* for *good* or a *B* for *bad* based on whether you think it will most likely cause you to attract money or to repel money. Once you're clear on what your conscious money beliefs are, you can begin to control which ones you keep, which ones you change, and which new ones you form. Your subconscious beliefs will tend to fall in line with your conscious beliefs.

4. Review the list monthly. Cross off old bad beliefs you've overcome and add new good beliefs you want to develop. This will lead to your beliefs becoming more and more productive.

5. Observe belief in action. To do this: listen to what people say (believe) about their lives and money; watch their dramas unfold; and see how their beliefs *give birth to* their circumstances.

6. When you hear or read facts or opinions about money or the economy, be aware of what beliefs they suggest. Embrace those beliefs you want to have and reject those you don't want.

WHAT OTHERS HAVE WRITTEN

What we believe to be true, what we believe
is possible, becomes what's true,
becomes what's possible.
—Anthony Robbins, *Unlimited Power,*
1986

Ironically, the abundance that shows up in
your life, or the lack of it, is directly
correlated to you and your beliefs.
—Eva Gregory, *The Feel Good Guide to Prosperity,*
2004

There are ... cases where a fact cannot come at all
unless a preliminary faith exists in its coming.
—William James, *The Will to Believe,* 1897

Life responds to us according to our beliefs ...
—Norman S. Lunde, *You Unlimited,* 1965

Knowledge of the powers of your subconscious mind
is the means to the royal road to riches of all kinds ...
—Dr. Joseph Murphy, *The Power of
Your Subconscious Mind,*
1963

If you can truly believe that you have received
something, your subconscious mind
will surely see that you get it.
—Dr. Venice J. Bloodworth, *Key to Yourself,*
1952

What you deeply, authentically Believe, you create.
—Brenda Anderson, *Playing the Quantum Field,* 2006

3

EXPECTANCY

Expectation is a powerful attractive force, because it draws things to you.

—Rhonda Byrne
The Secret, 2006

CONCEPTS AND COUNSEL

Expectancy is the state of assuming a certain something will come about. To assume a thing will come about is to *believe* it will. You tend to get what you expect—what you believe you will get—so, to get more money, expect to get more money.

To attract money using mind power, you must develop the subconscious belief that you already have the money you want. Until you *really* have your money, you will continue to send thoughts, feelings, and images of *not* having your money to your subconscious mind. Thus, you will undermine your subconscious belief.

Expectancy can help bridge the gap. Even though you know you don't yet have the money you want to have, you can believe you *will* have it. When you believe you'll have your money, you'll send thoughts, feelings, and images related to that belief to your subconscious. This flow of positive mental impressions will help ensure that, overall, your conscious thinking strengthens—not weakens—your subconscious belief that you have your money.

To help keep what you expect to come about aligned with what you want to bring about, know what you expect. Ask yourself from time to time, "What do I expect to happen about ...?" To know what you expect to happen is to know what you are creating. If you become aware that what you are creating is not what you want to bring about, change your expectations about what will be.

Know what you expect and expect what you want. When you align your expectations with your desired financial present and future, you and your money will always find each other.

SIMPLE STEPS

1. Under FINANCIAL EXPECTATIONS – FIVE YEARS, list what you have been expecting your financial situation—money, business, career, debt, and so on—to be then. For instance, you might have expected to be running a flower shop, to still be in debt, to be in the same job, to own a house, or to have $100,000 in the bank. Ten to fifteen items will give you a good idea of what you have been expecting.

2. Under FINANCIAL EXPECTATIONS – TEN YEARS, same as above.

3. Under FINANCIAL EXPECTATIONS – TWENTY YEARS, same thing.

4. Read over the three lists and think about what you've written. These expectations show you what you've been moving toward. Whether or not that was what you wanted, that was your most likely future—the future you've been creating with your mind.

5. Read the lists again. Cross off the expectations you'd like to exceed. You're on your way to creating expectations worthier of you. Cross off *all* your expectations if you want to.

6. Under WHAT I EXPECT, rewrite any expectations you haven't crossed off. Review the list now and then. Cross off those items which have come about and those which no longer live up to what you want. The better you get at using mind power to govern events, circumstances, and conditions, the greater your expectations will naturally become.

WHAT OTHERS HAVE WRITTEN

It is a well-defined and authentic principle that what
the mind profoundly expects it tends to receive.
—Norman Vincent Peale, *The Power
of Positive Thinking,*
1952

Man creates reality through expectation.
—Barbel Mohr, *The Cosmic Ordering Service*, 2001

Successful people expect the best and they generally
get it, because expectations have a way of
attracting to you their material equivalent.
—Tom Butler-Bowden, *50 Success Classics,*
2004

Expectation can be the triggering mechanism which
attracts into your life, every good you desire.
—Bob Proctor, *You Were Born Rich*, 1997

Expecting gives life and attracting
power to our desires.
—Mary Katherine MacDougall, *Prosperity Now,*
1969

You will never get any more out of
this life than you expect.
—Ben Sweetland, *I Can*, 1953

In your quiet thinking select your future, then accept it
as normal for you, and then expect it to happen.
—Raymond Charles Barker, *The Science
of Successful Living,*
1957

4

MONEY MINDSET

Fortunes gravitate to men whose minds have been prepared to attract them, just as surely as water gravitates to the ocean.

—Napoleon Hill
Think and Grow Rich, 1937

CONCEPTS AND COUNSEL

Your *money mindset* is the way you think and feel about money. It affects how you act with money and how money acts *with you*. Improve your money mindset, and you will attract more money.

Your money mindset includes your money-related desires, beliefs, and expectations. It also includes such things as your money-related resentments, regrets, and guilt. Your every thought and feeling regarding money is part of your money mindset.

Just by reading this book, you will greatly improve your money mindset. It's a good start, but there's more you can do.

Clear your mind of negative money-related emotions: let go of resentments toward anyone you feel got the best of you in a financial deal, stole from you, or didn't pay a debt to you; release your regrets for your money mistakes and missed opportunities; and let go of your guilt for money-related wrongs you've done others and for your own foolish money actions.

Have positive or neutral opinions about others' money: don't judge people for how they get, spend, save, invest, or give money; don't envy rich people or look down on poor people; and don't criticize the money practices of governments or businesses.

Act with positive or neutral feelings when you handle money: accept it gratefully; earn it happily; spend it confidently; give it joyfully; invest it hopefully; and lose it calmly.

By how you think, feel, and act, you mold that field of thought-energy that makes up your money mindset. The vibration of that energy then attracts or repels the money you desire.

SIMPLE STEPS

1. Under RESENTMENTS, list the people and incidents behind your money grudges: *Mr. Pike – sold me car with engine problems; Anthony – embezzled $7,000; Brenda – never paid back $100 loan.*

2. Review each resentment to see if the act was really as bad as you thought. See if perhaps there were factors you haven't allowed for. Whatever you decide, mentally forgive each person.

3. Under REGRETS, list those you have for your money mistakes and missed opportunities: *wish I'd taken Jones's offer; should have bought that house; shouldn't have invested in that stock.*

4. Review each regret to see if the mistakes were as bad as you thought and if the opportunities were as good as you thought. Whatever you decide, find something good about each incident—even if it's only that you gained insight or learned a lesson.

5. Under GUILT, list the money-related wrongs you've done to people and other money actions you have guilt over: *overcharged Mrs. Lee for that repair job; gambled away my inheritance.*

6. Review each guilt item to see if your actions were really as bad as you thought. Write down ways you might repay the people you feel you've wronged, and follow up on those ideas as you can. Whether or not you can repay everyone, forgive yourself.

WHAT OTHERS HAVE WRITTEN

Prosperity is created by a state of mind.
—Jack Canfield and Mark Victor Hansen,
Dare to Win, 1994

How you think about money determines
exactly what your financial reality is.
—Dr. Stuart Grayson, *The Ten Demandments
of Prosperity*, 1986

The mind is like a magnet, attracting and repelling,
and … its attractions and repulsions can
be determined by ourselves.
—Annie Besant, *Thought Power, Its
Control and Culture*, 1903

The circumstances and conditions of man's physical
world are the … effects of the active
elements in his mental world.
—C. D. Larson, *Mastery of Fate,*
1907

If people want to acquire money, they need to
develop a good money consciousness.
—Margaret R. Stortz, *Start Living
Every Day of Your Life,*
1981

Riches … correlate a rich mentality.
—Helen Wilmans, *The Conquest of Poverty*, 1899

Our ways of thinking make our happiness or
unhappiness, our success or non-success.
—H. Emilie Cady, *Lessons in Truth*, 1895

5

MONEY GOALS

Nothing happens, no forward steps
are taken until a goal is established.
Without goals individuals just
wander through life. They stumble
along, never knowing where
they are going, so they
never get anywhere.

—David J. Schwartz
The Magic of Thinking Big, 1959

CONCEPTS AND COUNSEL

A *money goal* is a specific monetary end you intend to bring about. You can use money goals to increase your income and net worth. Money goals tell your conscious and subconscious minds exactly what you want. This clear purpose impels you, and your subconscious, to find the means to *get* what you want.

With a better money mindset, you will attract more money whether or not you have money goals. Still, you should set money goals if you seek financial independence or great wealth.

A money goal should have a deadline, a target date for fulfillment. The deadline is crucial. If your goal is to have a million dollars, it will matter greatly to you whether it takes five years or thirty-five years for you to get the million.

A money goal takes on an immense, miraculous, and mysterious power when it is *written down*. This step is so vital that a money goal is not really a goal *unless* it is written down.

As you reach your money goals, you can set new, higher ones. Goal setting for money is an ongoing process. Knowing this, you should feel at ease about setting your money goals.

You can set more than one money goal at a time. For instance, you can set one- and five-year income goals and an eight-year net-worth goal. Find the mix that's right for you.

Money goals separate the prosperity dabblers from the serious wealth-seekers. Mind power is a dynamic *force* and, like any force, it must be focused to be put to productive use. Setting money goals is a key way to focus mind power to attract money.

SIMPLE STEPS

1. Under MY NEW LIFE, list what you'd have and do if you could afford to: *six-bedroom house, Porsche, motor home, send the kids to college, give money to parents and homeless shelter, travel.*

2. Think about how high an income and/or a net worth you would need to be able to have and do *all* the things you've listed.

3. Write amounts and deadlines for your first money goal(s): *$80,000 annual income by month/day/year; $10,000,000 net worth by m/d/y.*

4. On separate 3"x5" index cards, write each of your money goals as follows: *My goal is to be earning at least eighty thousand dollars ($80,000) yearly by m/d/y; My goal is to have a net worth of more than ten million dollars ($10,000,000) by m/d/y.*

5. Keep in mind you can adjust money goals up or down in amount and forward or backward in time. As a rule, don't change your money goals. Your subconscious mind works best with fixed targets.

6. Keep your money goals *secret.* This will help you conserve the power of your intentions, and it will shield you from negative feedback that might hurt your money mindset and subconscious belief. You can reveal a money goal to someone you believe will be supportive of your efforts to reach the goal, especially if the goal is to be a shared goal with that person.

WHAT OTHERS HAVE WRITTEN

One of the most essential things you need to do for
yourself is to choose a goal that is important to you.
—Les Brown, *Live Your Dreams*,
1992

How can you expect to become rich if you haven't
even decided what rich means to you?
—Tom Hopkins, *The Official Guide to Success*,
1982

It is difficult to stress ... the prime importance of a goal
as a necessary ingredient to success.
—Melvin Powers, *Dynamic Thinking*,
1955

No matter what you want to achieve ... write it down—
get a statement of your goal on paper.
—William E. Edwards, *Ten Days to a Great New Life*,
1963

Almost all successful people attribute their
success, at least in part, to goals.
—Alec Mackenzie, *Time for Success*,
1989

If you want to get rich, your goal has to be rich.
—T. Harv Eker, *Secrets of the Millionaire Mind*,
2005

It is impossible to advance properly
in life without goals.
—Og Mandino, *The Greatest Success in the World*,
1981

6

THINK END RESULTS

What you … need to know is,
What is the end result? Where do
you want to end up? What do
you want to create?

—Dr. Robert Anthony
*Dr. Robert Anthony's Advanced Formula
for Total Success*, 1988

CONCEPTS AND COUNSEL

With or without money goals, you will tend to try to figure out how to get the money you want. Your subconscious is better able to find the best ways. So, let it. For now, just relay to your subconscious the mental impressions of what you want. *Think end results.* The more you think about the end results you're striving for, the closer you are to achieving those results.

Don't worry about how you'll get your money. Don't spend a lot of time and energy trying to make more money in random ways. Relax. Be patient. Know your subconscious is hard at work.

You *can* try for a promotion on your job, look for a new job, or start a business. For now, do whatever you want to do, or feel you must do, to earn the money you need to live. But don't assume that's the way you'll reach your larger money goals.

If you choose to, write your novel. Study acting. Work on your invention. Do whatever else you think might bring you more money in the future. Do what you feel inclined to do but, again, don't assume that's the way you will reach your larger money goals. Those things *may* help you reach your larger money goals, but you don't want to limit your subconscious. You want to leave open all potential ways for your money to come to you.

By keeping your thoughts firmly on the end results you want, you strengthen your expectation that you'll get those results and your subconscious belief that you have those results. In time, your subconscious will find a good way for you to get your money. It will do what it has to do. You'll get your money.

SIMPLE STEPS

1. While reading them from the 3"x5" cards, repeat out loud, ten times each, any money goals you now have. Do this weekly.

2. Understand that to attract money using mind power, the thoughts of the end results you're after must be foremost in your mind. Think about those end results often during each day.

3. So that you may review any ideas you can come up with about how to get your money, list those ideas under POSSIBLE WAYS TO GET MY MONEY: *invest in real estate; freelance; sell insurance.*

4. Next to each item on your list, write *P* for *pleasant* or *U* for *unpleasant*, depending on whether or not you think you'd enjoy that activity. Put an *N* for *neutral* by some, if you like.

5. Cross off the unpleasant and neutral items. Number the pleasant ones from, more or less, the most pleasant down. Under PLEASANT WAYS TO GET MY MONEY, rewrite those items in order.

6. Study the list to see if one item seems to stand out from the others. If one item stands out, that may be your path. Or maybe you are already in a field you like and in which you might be able to make the money you want. If so, you may just have to improve your money mindset to get your money. You will know more once you have gone through Chapter 17, the chapter on right livelihood.

WHAT OTHERS HAVE WRITTEN

Constantly feed your mind a clear, vivid picture of
the ideal end result you're striving for.
—Tommy Newberry, *Success Is Not an Accident*,
1999

Have no attachment to the means by which
your desire will be delivered.
—Bob Doyle, *Wealth Beyond Reason*,
2003

When you choose your thoughts,
you choose results.
—Imelda Octavia Shanklin, *What Are You?*,
1929

The type of thought we entertain both creates and
draws conditions that crystallize about it ...
—Ralph Waldo Trine, *Character Building
Thought Power,* 1899

You get what you think about,
whether you want it or not.
—Esther and Jerry Hicks, *The Law of Attraction*, 2006

If you cling to a certain thought with dynamic will
power, it finally assumes a tangible outward form.
—Paramahansa Yogananda, *The Law of Success*,
1944

Our thought is the unseen magnet, ever attracting its
correspondence in things seen and tangible.
—Prentice Mulford, *Thoughts Are Things*,
1889

7

THINK AND FEEL AS IF

What you put into your mind in the nature of your thoughts and feelings …is what subsequently materializes for you in your outer world.

—Harold Sherman
The New TNT, Miraculous Power Within You, 1966

CONCEPTS AND COUNSEL

Your subconscious mind causes your finances to be what you think they are and what you think they will be. To govern your finances using mind power, *think as if* the end results you desire are now or will be reality. And, just as importantly, avoid thinking about financial circumstances you don't want to bring about.

By what you think, you tell your subconscious what to create. Your emotions give your subconscious the *power* to create. Thus, it's as crucial for you to *feel as if* about your finances as it is for you to think as if about them. Since thought often gives rise to feeling, thinking as if leads to feeling as if.

So, by being aware of your feelings, you can know how well you're thinking as if. When you really think as if your finances are and will be the way you want them to be, you'll have feelings such as happiness and excitement. Feelings such as fear and doubt will show you that you're not *really* thinking as if.

Negative emotions can affect your subconscious as powerfully as positive emotions. Thoughts of things you *don't* want to come about, mixed with *fear* of those things coming about, will give your subconscious the pattern and the power to attract and create those feared things. And by mixing *doubt* with thoughts of things you *want* to create, you cancel positive emotions and deplete power your subconscious needs to create what you want.

By thinking and feeling as if you have and will have your money—*more* than you think and feel as if you don't have and won't have your money—you cause yourself to get your money.

SIMPLE STEPS

1. Under HOW THINGS ARE, list the major facts of your present financial circumstances: *I earn $3,650 per month; I owe about $6,400 on my credit cards; I have $350 in my savings account; my net worth is minus $11,000.* Approximate figures will do.

2. Under HOW I'D LIKE THINGS TO BE, rewrite the above statements to reflect what you'd choose the facts to be: *I'd earn $7,000 per month; my credit cards would be paid off; I'd have $50,000 in savings; I'd have a net worth of $3,000,000.*

3. Relax. Breathe deeply. Contemplate how you'd think and feel if the items on your HOW I'D LIKE THINGS TO BE list were true.

4. Begin now to think and feel as if what you wrote has come about. Using examples from above, you'd go through each day thinking and feeling as if you earn $7,000 a month or have a net worth of $3,000,000. In your mind, those things would be true.

5. Review your HOW THINGS ARE list monthly to see what your situation is at that time. Update your figures. Write down some ideas about how to make more progress in the coming month.

6. Review and update your HOW I'D LIKE THINGS TO BE list monthly. See how well you've been thinking and feeling as if the listed items were true. Note some ways you can do better.

WHAT OTHERS HAVE WRITTEN

Your outer world of form and experience is a
reflection of your inner world of thoughts and feelings.
—John Randolph Price, *The Abundance Book*, 1987

... the way each of us thinks and feels about
our money is the key factor in determining
how much we ultimately have.
—Suze Orman, *The Courage to Be Rich*,
1999

When you know what you want, all you really
have to do is think it and feel it.
—Joe Vitale, *The Attractor Factor*, 2005

Whenever you think and feel, consciousness
is in action for good or for bad.
—Ervin Seale, *Ten Words That Will
Change Your Life*, 1954

When our thinking and feeling are wrong—then
we make it ... impossible for "things" to
work correctly on the "outside."
—Charles M. Simmons, *Your Subconscious Power*,
1965

Take control of your thoughts and your feelings,
for they are the blueprints of your life.
—Herbert Harris, *The Twelve Universal Laws
of Success*, 2004

When we think, we create. When we feel, we create.
Dr. Donald Curtis, *Science of Mind in Daily Living*,
1975

8

SPEAK AS IF

There is tremendous power in
our words, and many of us
are not aware of just how
important they are.

—Louise L. Hay
The Power Is Within You, 1991

CONCEPTS AND COUNSEL

Spoken words set in motion and direct subconscious power. So, you should use great care when you speak, just as when you think. To attract money using mind power, *speak as if* what you want to be true about your finances either is now or will be true.

What you say reveals the way you think. You might assume you "think positive" about your life and about your finances. Still, your unguarded words will expose the way you *really* think. If you're not speaking as if, you're not thinking as if.

What you say *affects* the way you think. Your words mold your conscious and subconscious beliefs. So, what you say about your finances, you cause. Speak of lack and poverty, and you get them. Speak of abundance and wealth, and you get *them*.

Your subconscious mind translates your words into the images it uses to create. By saying "I don't want to lose money on that deal," you cause your subconscious to form images of you losing money and to work toward that end. But by saying you want to *make* money on the deal, you cause your subconscious to form images of you *making* money and to work toward *that* end. Be aware of the sorts of images your words are likely to call forth.

For you, speaking should not be just a careless, aimless process in which you say whatever happens to come to your mind. Instead, speaking should be a mindful, purposeful process in which you think before you speak, say what you mean, and voice what you want to make real.

Speaking as if about your finances will improve the way you *think* about money. It will improve the way you *attract* money.

SIMPLE STEPS

1. As a helpful reminder, write SPEAK AS IF on a 3"x5" index card. Put the card somewhere you'll see it at least once daily.

2. Under HOW I SPEAK NOW, list some negative money-related phrases you're in the habit of using: *I can't afford that/It's too expensive; I don't make enough money; Business is slow.*

3. Under A BETTER WAY TO SPEAK, rewrite the negative phrases from the above list into positive or neutral phrases: *I'm not going to buy that; I make plenty of money; Business is good.*

4. Work on speaking less in line with your HOW I SPEAK NOW list and more in line with your A BETTER WAY TO SPEAK list.

5. Review both lists monthly to see how well you're doing and how you can do better. Add and delete items as you progress.

6. You can't just go around telling everyone you are a wealthy philanthropist who lives in a mansion. So, try to find at least one person open to using the speak-as-if technique. Speak as if with each other: *I'm debt free; I'm rich; My book is a bestseller; I got a raise; My new house has a pool; I am financially free; Money flows to me easily; I made my first million.* Make a game of it, but remember it's *not* a game. It's part of the process you're using to manifest your desired financial future.

WHAT OTHERS HAVE WRITTEN

If we listen to the words of the failure multitude we
will soon learn that by their words they
are justified and condemned.
—Julia Seton, *The Science of Success*, 1914

The laws of mind go into operation
through our words.
—Georgiana Tree West, *Prosperity's
Ten Commandments*, 1944

Thoughts are living things, and spoken words give
to thoughts a body of physical vibrations
which makes them still stronger.
—Walter DeVoe, *Mystic Words of Mighty Power*, 1905

Words ... constitute a point of focus
for creative energy.
—William E. Towne, *Health and Wealth from Within*, 1909

Words are a powerful factor in your life; use
them wisely, and you will recreate all
the conditions about you.
—Louise B. Brownell, *Life Abundant for You*, 1928

Talk only about the things you want
to see live and grow.
—Eric Butterworth, *Spiritual Economics*, 1983

Your spoken word goes to the ends of the universe
and is returned to you—and it doesn't return to you
empty. It comes back ... full to overflowing with
that which you decree and declare.
—Edwene Gaines, *The Four Spiritual
Laws of Prosperity*, 2005

9

ACT AS IF

Live as if it were already manifest
and you shall find it manifest.

—Henry Harrison Brown
*How to Control Fate
through Suggestion*, 1901

CONCEPTS AND COUNSEL

The conscious and subconscious minds are greatly influenced by action. When you *act as if* your money is on the way or already in the bank, you strengthen your expectation that you'll get the money and your subconscious belief that you have the money.

When you act as if, you don't let doubt about getting the money you want, or fear of not having enough money in the future, keep you from spending or giving money in reasonable ways.

If you knew you would get your money, as you'd know it if you'd won a lottery jackpot, you'd likely be freer with your money right now. For instance, you might buy that new refrigerator you need, update your wardrobe, or give an expensive gift.

If you won a lottery jackpot, you would likely do certain things before receiving the money. For instance, you might test drive new cars, plan an extended vacation, or open a money market account to deposit your winnings into.

If you won the lottery, you would likely, if you were wise, learn what you could about how to manage a lot of money. For instance, you might read up on personal finance and investing, take a money management course, or talk to a financial advisor.

Since you don't have your money yet, there are limits—but much of what you would do if you knew you'd get your money, and if you had your money, is what you should be doing now.

By acting as if concerning your money, you strengthen your expectancy and belief and call up and focus your subconscious power in ways you can only do by taking deliberate physical action.

SIMPLE STEPS

1. Make a study of personal finance. Learn about things such as insurance, income taxes, retirement planning, and estate planning.

2. Under PERSONAL FINANCE, list ideas you get from your research about things to do and subjects to study further. Number the items in the order you want to do them. Start doing them.

3. Make a study of investing. Learn about investments such as certificates of deposit, various securities, mutual funds, stocks, bonds, real estate, precious metals, and other investments as you like.

4. Under INVESTING, list ideas you get from your research about things to do and subjects to study further. Number the items in the order you want to do them. Start doing them.

5. Under ACT AS IF, list ways you would act now if you knew for sure that you would get your money and if you already had your money: *eat out more often*; *be more at ease about money*; *hire fitness trainer*; *buy new house*; *follow stock market*; *quit job*; *get Mom new car*; *have the property landscaped*; *take up golf*; *go on cruise*; *visit home*.

6. Cross off the listed items you can't or shouldn't do now—such as buying a new house or quitting your job—and begin to act in the remaining ways you've listed. Review the list monthly to see how well you're acting as if. Note how you can do better. Do Better.

WHAT OTHERS HAVE WRITTEN

If you want to achieve something that has always
eluded you ... act as if it were already here.
—Dr. Wayne W. Dyer, *Real Magic,*
1992

... act as if your desire were already manifested.
—U. S. Andersen, *The Magic in Your Mind,*
1961

You should ... begin building your expectancy and
faith in financial independence by studying the subject
of finance, economics, and investments.
—Catherine Ponder, *The Dynamic
Laws of Prosperity,*
1962

Act wealthy.
—Annie Rix Militz, *Both Riches and Honor,*
1945

Acting as if you are wealthy is a powerful tool
for attracting what you desire.
—Lynn A. Robinson, *Real Prosperity,*
2004

Act as if it were impossible to fail.
—Dorothea Brande, *Wake Up and Live!,*
1936

All the power of the universe is with you. Feel it,
know it, and then act as though it were true.
—Ernest Holmes, *The Science of Mind,*
1938

10

AFFIRMATIONS

Not only do affirmations impress
the subconscious mind thus
producing action in accordance with
the Will, but they project outwards
from the mind into space, attract
forces and help from other
sources and bring them to
minister and to bless.

—Henry Thomas Hamblin
Dynamic Thought, 1921

CONCEPTS AND COUNSEL

An *affirmation* is a word, phrase, or sentence designed and used to methodically instill in the subconscious mind the mental impressions of the way you want your circumstances to develop.

Affirmations can be thought, spoken, or written. They can be used to affect what you are, what you do, what you have, and what happens to you: *I am a great salesperson*; *I always make good financial decisions*; *I have $100,000 in the bank*; *Good investment opportunities always come my way*.

Form your affirmations in the present tense—affirm that what you want is *already* true, not that it *will be* true. Affirm the end results you want but not how you achieved those results. Make your affirmations specific, clear, and brief. Make them count.

Repeat affirmations from a few times to dozens of times in a row. Do them with strong, positive feelings. Though you'll likely do most of them mentally, state some verbally each day. As you see fit, write out the most meaningful and pressing ones.

Do affirmations upon waking and just before sleep, when the subconscious is most receptive to suggestion. Do them while you clean house, walk, shower, and so on. Do your most important and urgent ones often each day, and do others as you want to. As a safeguard against undesirable outcomes, you can end an affirmation set by voicing or thinking this: *This or something better with only good for all concerned*.

Using affirmations is an easy way to mold your subconscious belief. Affirmations work in the steady, focused way needed to cause your subconscious to bring you and your money together.

SIMPLE STEPS

1. Under MY PRESENT FINANCIAL CONCERNS, list those you have: *I don't have next month's rent money yet*; *I need money to buy a nice-looking, good-running car*; *I lost the lease on my shop.*

2. Write an affirmation for each concern: *I always pay my rent on time*; *I own a nice-looking, good-running car*; *My shop is in the perfect location.* Do these affirmations often each day.

3. Write an affirmation for each item on your HOW I'D LIKE THINGS TO BE list (Chapter 7): *I earn at least $7,000 monthly*; *My credit card balances are all zero*; *I have $50,000 in savings.* Do these affirmations daily.

4. Write affirmations for any written money goals you have: *I earn at least $80,000 yearly*; *I have more than $10,000,000 in assets.* Do these affirmations daily.

5. Daily, in a special notebook, while saying them, write your money-goal affirmations once each as follows: *I earn at least eighty thousand dollars ($80,000) yearly*; *I have more than ten million dollars ($10,000,000) in assets.* Date your entries.

6. Under MY AFFIRMATIONS, list those you've written down so far. Review the list monthly. Cross off the affirmations you'll no longer be using and write any new ones you will be using.

WHAT OTHERS HAVE WRITTEN

Affirmation is the beginning of change,
the beginning of creating destiny.
—Sandra Anne Taylor, *Quantum Success*,
2006

Affirmations are one way of attuning your
subconscious so that it will move you steadily
and surely toward your goal.
—Ruth Drury, *Tapping Into Prosperity*,
1991

Affirmations ... when properly understood, and
applied, will totally transform your future.
—Sandy Forster, *How to Be Wildly Wealthy Fast*,
2004

Affirm as though you already have what you want ...
—John-Roger and Peter McWilliams, *Life 101*,
1991

Used wisely, affirmations can be powerful tools ...
—Roy Hunter, *Success Through Mind Power*,
1986

By repeating an affirmation over and over again, it
becomes embedded in the subconscious mind,
and eventually becomes your reality.
—Stuart Wilde, *Affirmations*,
1987

With affirmations, your potential is unlimited.
—Brian Tracy, *Maximum Achievement*,
1993

11

VISUALIZATION

Through our inner images, our mind is causing what happens to us *all the time.* Whatever we experience in our lives … is the direct result of these images.

—Adelaide Bry with Marjorie Bair
Visualization: Directing the Movies of Your Mind, 1978

CONCEPTS AND COUNSEL

Visualization is the act of willfully forming mental images. To affect material reality using visualization, form images for your subconscious mind to use as patterns to work from.

A visualized image can be *still* or *moving*: a new car parked in your driveway; you driving a new car. An image can be *detailed* or *vague*: a blue 1965 Ford Mustang; a faint outline of a car.

You can visualize from the *inside- or outside-your-body* point of view: you can imagine you are at your desk, signing a check; you can imagine *watching* yourself sign that check.

You can visualize while reclining, with your eyes closed, for a few minutes or longer. You can visualize (imagine) while standing or walking, with your eyes open, for even a few seconds at a time.

Visualize with positive feelings. Do it just before sleep. Do it just after waking, while still deeply relaxed. Do it other times. To add focus and power, do some related affirmations as you visualize. Visualize *only* what you want to experience. As you see fit, after visualizing, voice or think this: *This or something better with only good for all concerned.*

Images are always forming in your conscious and subconscious minds, so you can attract more money without *trying* to form images. And visualization can have drawbacks: images you form might keep better things away; images you form might be of things not in harmony with your highest best good. Still, used with care, visualization can help you attract and create almost any circumstances you can imagine and believe you can bring about.

SIMPLE STEPS

1. With eyes closed, imagine a chair. Whether or not you feel you "saw" anything, the impression or image you got shows the way *you* visualize. Your way is right for you. Practice, and you'll learn to create more distinct impressions and/or images.

2. Sit or lie comfortably with eyes closed and be aware as you breathe deeply from your abdomen. Release the tension from your body. When you can, use this or another method to deeply relax before visualizing. Other times, just go ahead and form the images.

3. With eyes open, imagine some aspects of how things will be when you have the money you want. Do this throughout each day.

4. With your eyes closed, see yourself, from outside your imagined body, standing in your kitchen talking to a family member. Now see from inside your imagined body—see that family member looking back at you. You can use both of these techniques as you choose, but try to visualize mostly from the *inside*-your-body point of view.

5. Practice combining the still, moving, detailed, vague, and inside- and outside-your-body techniques. Find what works best for you.

6. Visualize the financial end results you want. Once you know the tasks you'll be doing to help get those results, visualize yourself doing those tasks well and overcoming obstacles you feel you may have to face to do so (using the inside-your-body technique).

WHAT OTHERS HAVE WRITTEN

Manifestation through creative visualization is the
process of realizing and making visible
on the physical plane our divine potential.
—Shakti Gawain, *Creative Visualization*,
1978

... you can be, do, and have whatever
you can imagine.
—Neale Donald Walsch, *Conversations with God*,
1995

Visualization ... makes accessible for the first
time really magical principles that until
now were only available to a few.
—Chris Odle, *Practical Visualization*,
1990

You can create what you want in life; first you have
to imagine it clearly. Imagine your ideal scene.
—Marc Allen, *The Millionaire Course*, 2003

... you must always keep a mental
image of your goal.
—Chuck Norris, *The Secret of Inner Strength*, 1988

We all possess more power and greater possibilities
than we realize, and visualizing is one of
the greatest of these powers.
—Genevieve Behrend, *Your Invisible Power*, 1921

Every day—every few hours—see
your vision materializing.
—Sylvester Stallone, *Sly Moves*, 2005

12

ENVIRONMENT

Everyone must be accountable for creating their own personal environment for success.
As a successful person matures, they take more and more responsibility for...
their environment.

—Don Hutson, Chris Crouch, and George Lucas
The Contented Achiever: How to Get What You Want and Love What You Get, 2001

CONCEPTS AND COUNSEL

Your *environment* consists of all you see and hear on a regular basis. It reflects your thinking—you create, attract, and are drawn to what you think about most often. And your environment *affects* your thinking— your conscious and subconscious thoughts tend to fall in line with what you normally see and hear.

Think about what you *do* see and hear on a typical day. Think about your home and your workplace. Think about the other places you frequent. Think about the activities you engage in.

Consider the thoughts that reach you from other people. Family, friends, acquaintances, coworkers, and strangers often express negative thoughts of poverty and lack which can be harmful to your money mindset. They express these thoughts to you in many ways including: in person, by phone, through letters; in books, magazines, and newspapers; on TV, radio, and the Internet; and even just *mentally*.

By thinking about which aspects of your environment might be helpful and which harmful to your efforts to attract more money, you begin to see where you need to make improvements.

Although you should act on outer conditions to improve them, always keep in mind that your outer environment is the effect of your inner environment. So, your daily thoughts, affirmations, and visualizations should reflect the environment you *want*.

When you improve your outer environment, you will, as a direct result, improve the stimulus reaching your subconscious mind day after day. In this way, you will help your subconscious to work toward your money goals in a more direct and efficient manner. And you will thrive financially and in other ways, too.

SIMPLE STEPS

1. Under MY NEGATIVE ENVIRONMENTAL FACTORS, list the main elements you think may be harmful to your money-getting efforts: *I spend too much time reading romance novels*; *Robert voices a lot of pessimistic thoughts*; *I live in a rundown neighborhood.*

2. Under MY POSITIVE ENVIRONMENTAL FACTORS, list the main elements you think are helpful to your money-getting efforts: *Lisa encourages me to strive and to grow*; *My support group seems to be helping*; *My office is in an impressive building.*

3. Review the above two lists and, under WAYS TO IMPROVE MY ENVIRONMENT, list any suggestions you can come up with at this time: *Read fewer novels and more self-help books*; *Avoid Robert as often as I can*; *Move to a nicer neighborhood*; *Spend more time with Lisa*; *Attend my support group more often*; *Frame an inspiring quote for my desk at work.* Begin making these improvements right away.

4. Review the above three lists monthly. Add new items you can think of and cross off those you no longer need to refer to.

5. With broom, rag, screwdriver, hammer, and rake, tune up your present surroundings. This will help you tune up your thinking.

6. Do something each day to improve your environment. Even one small action a day will have a major impact in a short time.

WHAT OTHERS HAVE WRITTEN

… once a man has created by his thought an
environment, that environment must
surround him sooner or later.
—Dr. L. W. de Laurence, *The Master Key*, 1914

There are two classes of folks in this world;
those who will be trained by environment,
and those who train environment.
—Harriet Luella McCollum, *What Makes a Master?*,
1932

The great nature makes its own environment …
—Ella Wheeler Wilcox, *Heart of the New Thought*,
1902

Your understanding must mould your activities and
your environment; you must not allow
your environment to mould you.
—Emmet Fox, *Power through Constructive Thinking*,
1932

Our environment reflects conditions corresponding to
the predominant mental attitude which we entertain.
—Charles F. Haanel, *The Master Key System*, 1917

… make sure that you control your environment.
—W. Clement Stone, *The Success System
That Never Fails*, 1962

Whatever your present environment may be,
you will fall, remain, or rise with your
thoughts, your Vision, your Ideal.
—James Allen, *As a Man Thinketh*, 1902

13

ORGANIZATION

If you want to be rich, you must be orderly. All men with great wealth are orderly—and order is Heaven's first law.

—Florence Scovel Shinn
*The Game of Life
and How to Play It*, 1925

CONCEPTS AND COUNSEL

Organization is the state of being organized. It requires and breeds efficiency and purpose. It involves sorting things out. It calls for structure. When organized, you're better able to focus your mind power and actions to get the money you want.

To attract money using mind power, you organize your thoughts in a certain way. This prompts you to begin organizing your environment and affairs. *This* then causes your thoughts to become even more organized—the effects run both ways.

Simplify your life, and you'll be better able to keep it organized. This may entail choosing personal freedom over approval, self-restraint over indulgence, quality over quantity, less over more, none over any, and letting go over holding on.

To organize your home and other personal spaces, go through your clothes, housewares, photos, and paperwork. Everything. Get rid of what you don't use, want, or need and organize the rest.

To help organize your activities: manage your time; limit your commitments and actions to those that matter most to you; keep daily, weekly, monthly, and yearly to-do lists; and prioritize.

It's not enough to just know what you want to do, you need to *schedule* many of your activities. For instance, if you have to write a report, decide on a date and time to do it. If it will take several sessions to do the report, schedule them.

Your money-getting efforts start with your thinking. Your environment and affairs mirror and affect your thinking, so they should be organized and purposeful, not random and aimless.

SIMPLE STEPS

1. Start to-do lists for this week, this month, and this year. List whatever you can think of at the moment: *buy personal finance book*; *research XYZ stock*; *get estimates for new fence*. Schedule those items you can. At the end of each week, month, and year, start your next list. Add to these lists as needed.

2. Nightly, list the top six tasks you'd like to do the next day. Number them from the most important, hard to do, or urgent on down. The next day do, in order, the tasks you can get to.

3. Schedule time each week to keep up on personal and financial matters: pay bills; check account balances; write letters; make phone calls; schedule appointments; review and act on mail.

4. Schedule time each week to begin cleaning and organizing your personal spaces. Go through every closet, drawer, cabinet, box, and folder. Get rid of what you can and tidy up the rest.

5. Once you *get* organized, *stay* organized. Each week, straighten up and clean up. Each month, review your personal spaces and your affairs, give away or discard objects, and organize as needed.

6. Right now, empty your purse or wallet. Get rid of the gum wrappers and other useless items. Put back in only what you need and make sure you *have* all you need. Do this weekly.

WHAT OTHERS HAVE WRITTEN

The fastest, most efficient, easiest and best
way of doing *anything*, including
thinking, is the organized way.
—Harry Lorayne, *Secrets of Mind Power*,
1961

Clean up and organize your life and your
space, and watch your life expand.
—Allen Rosenthal, *Your Mind the Magician*,
1991

To simplify is to bring order, clarity,
and purpose into our lives.
—Duane Elgin, *Voluntary Simplicity*,
1981

It is your duty to order your life well
in every single act ...
—Marcus Aurelius, *Meditations*, 2nd Century

The order of the physical environment is a
reflection of the order or state of the mind.
—Iyanla Vanzant, *One Day My Soul Just Opened Up*,
1998

Simplicity, simplicity, simplicity!
—Henry David Thoreau, *Walden*,
1854

Disorderly persons are rarely rich,
and orderly persons are rarely poor.
—Samuel Smiles, *Thrift*,
1885

14

LAWS OF MONEY

There are certain laws that govern
the acquisition of riches; once these
laws are mastered and applied,
riches follow with
mathematical certainty.

—Robert A. Russell
You Too Can Be Prosperous:
Studies in Prosperity, 1950

CONCEPTS AND COUNSEL

Money moves according to certain natural tendencies—or universal laws. When you align your thoughts and actions with these *laws of money*, you become an attractive point for money.

Money goes where it flows: circulating money attracts money; stagnant money repels money and invites loss. So, for instance, it's better to spend or give money wisely than to hoard it fearfully, better to put it in the bank than in a home safe.

Money goes where it's welcome. So, by your actions, show the universe you're open to receiving. Two examples: if you see a penny on the ground, pick it up; accept money gifts—and all gifts—graciously.

Money goes where it's appreciated. So, be grateful for all the money you've had in the past, for all the money you have now, and for all the money you'll have in the future.

Money goes where it's respected. So, spend wisely, save and invest carefully, pay bills on time, keep good financial records, and get professional help and advice when you need it.

Money goes where it's given out from. So, give the universe back part of what you receive. The age-old practice of tithing is fundamental. Some say the tithe (ten percent of one's income) should be given to the source of one's spiritual support; but others say the tithe can go to any good causes. Decide what you believe and tithe accordingly. You can give in less consistent ways than tithing, but ideally that should be *in addition to* your tithing.

You control how money moves through your life. When you work *with* the laws of money, you will have all the money you want and need.

SIMPLE STEPS

1. Under MY MONEY BLOCKS, list ways you block your money flow: *I don't keep accurate financial records*; *I make impulsive purchases*; *I pay bills late*. Review and revise the list monthly.

2. Under REMOVING MY MONEY BLOCKS, list ways to help yourself remove your blocks: *Keep better financial records*; *Make shopping lists and stick to them*; *Pay bills within two days of getting them*. Review and revise the list monthly. Notice your progress.

3. Under MY BLESSINGS, list the major things you have to be grateful for: *family, friends, health, home, job, savings account, investment income, education*. Review and add to this list at least monthly and give thanks daily for your blessings.

4. Under MONTHLY SPENDING, list figures for food, rent, phone, utilities, transportation, entertainment, clothing, reading materials, insurance, and so on. If you find any wasteful spending, make notes about how to lessen it. Follow through.

5. Under SAVINGS, INVESTMENTS, AND INSURANCE, list any you have. At least yearly, review the list to see if your money is in the best places. List changes you want to make. Make them.

6. Decide what percentage of your income you will start giving regularly and to what organizations and/or people. Give it.

WHAT OTHERS HAVE WRITTEN

Basic laws are always in operation to
establish your prosperity, or lack of it.
—Winifred Wilkinson, *Miracle Power for Today*,
1969

Dare to give freely and receive freely.
—Jack and Cornelia Addington, *Your Needs Met*, 1966

Make no expense but to do good to others
or yourself; i.e., waste nothing.
—Benjamin Franklin, *Autobiography*, 1790

... when we mail a check to any philanthropy,
benevolence, or charity, it is like mailing
it to our own bank account.
—Joel S. Goldsmith, *Invisible Supply*,
1983

There is nothing comparable to the drawing power of
gratitude in attracting the good things of life to us.
—Rellimeo, *Within the Holy of Holies*,
1920

Tithing is based on a law that cannot fail, and it is the
surest way ever found to demonstrate plenty ...
—Charles Fillmore, *Prosperity*,
1936

When we give, we simply make
room for more to come in.
—Lenedra J. Carroll, *The Architecture
of All Abundance*,
2001

15

INTUITION

What is called intuition is absolute
within its own right and dominion.
It is your complete and motivating
existence on the earth.

—Ernest L. Norman
*The Infinite Concept
of Cosmic Creation*, 1956

CONCEPTS AND COUNSEL

Intuition is direct knowing without reasoning. It works beyond and is a better guide than conscious thought. Other terms for it are instinct, ESP, and sixth sense. Through intuition, your subconscious mind can reveal to you key knowledge and insights.

Many of the mind-power techniques you're now learning will help you influence your subconscious with mental impressions of what you want. With intuition, you'll let your subconscious influence *you* by showing you the ways to *get* what you want.

You can invite intuition by being open to it. Intuitive insights can come at any time, though they tend, also, to come at *certain* times, such as upon waking. When intuitive insights do come, don't resist, question, or judge them; *do* study the thoughts, feelings, and images that are coming in. Also, intuitive insights come in dreams. Look to your dreams for information, understanding, and guidance.

You can strengthen intuition by acting on it. You will get signs—thoughts, feelings, images, dreams—showing which people and situations are right for you and which are wrong for you. Do your best to see these signs. Do your best to follow them.

Through its fixed linkage with Universal Mind, with all minds, and with your higher self, your subconscious knows things you can't consciously know. Its guidance is based, in part, on knowledge of events occurring at a distance, knowledge of the past and future, and knowledge of the thoughts and actions of others.

Cultivate, trust, rely on, and act on your intuition, and it will help you find your way to the worthwhile things you seek in life, including plenty of money.

SIMPLE STEPS

1. To capture your intuitive insights before you forget them, always keep pen and paper or a small recorder with you and by your bed. Record ideas when they come and dreams upon waking.

2. To get your subconscious to work on a question or problem, first clearly state it in writing. Then learn all you can about the subject or issue. Next, contemplate the matter from all angles. Finally, put the matter out of your mind. Let it go.

3. To get your insights, wait for and expect guidance. To try to get results sooner, relax, reflect on your issue, and see if information shows up. When fitting, evaluate and verify what you get. When you can, just have faith in what you get and show that faith through action.

4. Before falling asleep each night, reflect on any issues you want insight into. Upon waking, reflect on the same issues again and be keenly alert for whatever impressions may come to you.

5. Know that when information comes, it may be the final answer you've been looking for or only a part of the whole. Take action as you are guided to.

6. When you feel an intuitive urge to act, you will not always know what the action relates to. Get used to not always knowing why you're doing what you're doing. Get in the habit of acting more from your intuitive feelings and less from your conscious reasoning.

WHAT OTHERS HAVE WRITTEN

Intuition does not reason, nor does it
need to. Intuition simply knows.
—Laura Day, *Practical Intuition*,
1996

... the gift of intuitive power is available to all
of us when we are open to receive it.
—Marta Hiatt, Ph.D., *Mind Magic*,
2001

Learn to listen to your inner guidance.
—Sanaya Roman and Duane Packer,
Creating Money, 1988

We lie in the lap of immense intelligence,
which makes us receivers of its truth
and organs of its activities.
—Ralph Waldo Emerson, *Self-Reliance*,
1841

Intuition ... is clearly one of the most important
areas to develop in your life if you
are interested in success ...
—Lee Milteer, *Feel and Grow Rich*, 1993

The intuition serves as a bridge between your
conscious self and the Infinite Intelligence,
the life force of all creation.
—Dale W. Olson, *Knowing Your Intuitive Mind*,
1990

Trust your heart, especially when it is a strong one.
—Baltasar Gracian, *The Art of Worldly Wisdom*, 1647

16

PLANS

By putting together a plan in much the same way as you would use a road map—by being systematic and studying the various alternatives—you focus the direction of your thoughts and find yourself capable of reaching almost any goal you please.

—John Marks Templeton
Discovering the Laws of Life, 1994

CONCEPTS AND COUNSEL

A *plan* is a detailed, spelled-out way to do something. A plan gives you a potential way to reach a goal. Planning can provide a bridge between your thinking and your doing. At some point, you should have a separate written plan for reaching each of your money goals.

To reach your big money goals, you'll likely need to achieve certain other aims first. By writing out a plan for each of these subgoals, you'll help insure you *know* what you need to do, and that you *do* what you need to do, to reach your big goals.

Just as your money goals should have deadlines, many of your subgoals should have deadlines as well. Deadlines will move you and your subconscious mind to act. Your deadlines should be far enough off to give you time to work your plans, but they should not be so far-off that you can get away with being lazy. If, at some point in the process, you decide you will need more time to reach one of your goals, you can extend your deadline for that goal.

You likely won't know all the tasks you'll need to do to reach a given goal; you'll gain knowledge as you go along. So, review your plans regularly and adjust them as you need to. By doing this, you'll be better able to keep yourself on course.

Written plans can help you focus your mind power and your actions. Written plans can show you what to do to pursue your goals. By writing things down, you make them clear to yourself and to your subconscious. If what you intend to do is clear to you and your subconscious, and you keep revising and working your plans, nothing can keep you from reaching your big money goals.

SIMPLE STEPS

1. At the top of separate clean sheets of paper, write each of your money goals just as you wrote them on the index cards (Chapter 5).

2. Over time, think about ways to reach your money goals. Be open to intuitive guidance. Do needed research. As you decide on steps to reaching a goal, write them on the correct list.

3. Once you have the basic elements of a plan, number the items in a logical order. Rewrite those items under a new heading: *My Plan for Earning $120,000 Yearly by m/d/y*. You will then have a tangible plan for reaching one of your money goals.

4. As you see fit, write separate plans for the steps in your money-goal plans. Suppose you want to start a weekend swap meet business as part of your income-goal plan. To reach that subgoal, you might need to visit swap meets, get a business license, and find suppliers. You could list these tasks under a heading: *My Plan for Having a Swap Meet Business by m/d/y*.

5. Review your plans monthly: add and cross off items; adjust your deadlines; abandon plans; make new plans as needed; and so on.

6. Come up with and use affirmations for each major subgoal: *My swap meet business clears me more than $50,000 yearly*. Visualize those goals as though they were achieved.

WHAT OTHERS HAVE WRITTEN

When you begin to actually work toward
your goals through a plan of action,
you assert power over your life.
—Stedman Graham, *You Can Make It Happen*,
1997

Your road to success requires planning.
—Mack R. Douglas, *How to Make a
Habit of Succeeding*, 1966

… before you take action, you have to know what
you want and have a plan to accomplish it.
—Bill Stiles, *Mind Power to Success*,
1986

A plan … helps you strategize about how you
are going to get from point A to point B.
—Richard Carlson, Ph.D., *Don't Worry, Make Money*,
1997

Your plans should always lead to the attainment of
your goals. This is the stuff success is made of.
—Scott Alexander, *Rhinoceros Success*, 1980

You must have a plan of action to
reach your monetary goals.
—Gary R. McMonagle, *Instant Money*,
1991

When we focus our minds on our plans of action,
we program ourselves for success.
—Dr. John F. Demartini, *Count Your Blessings*,
1997

17

RIGHT LIVELIHOOD

Right Livelihood is an idea about work which is linked to the natural order of things.

—Dr. Marsha Sinetar
Do What You Love, The Money Will Follow: Discovering Your Right Livelihood, 1987

CONCEPTS AND COUNSEL

Right livelihood is work in line with one's natural abilities and talents, deep interests, and passions. To move toward lasting wealth, and to attain real success, find your right livelihood, take time to grow into it, and devote your working life to it.

You'll tend to do best in, and most enjoy working in, those fields you're best suited to and most drawn to. You can earn money in other ways, but you won't be fulfilled. What you do for money should increase, not lessen, your quality of life.

They may well be the same, but if you must choose between work you feel best suited to and work you most want to do, do the latter. With enough desire (power), you can overcome lack of natural ability or talent and do well in the field you choose.

Until you find your right livelihood, your life won't be complete and you won't find lasting peace. Once you've found your work, remain open-minded. Your right livelihood may change during your life, and earlier work may prepare you for a new calling.

Strive to express your natural abilities and talents. Follow your deep interests and passions. Whether or not you can earn money doing it at this time, honor your nature. Do what you must to pay the bills but, also, do what you're good at, do what you're drawn to, do what you love doing. The money will come.

To win *true* success in this life, you must add value to the world by serving people in the way you were meant to. You'll find that way by doing what the universe prompts you to do. You'll find your right livelihood—and your rightful place in the world.

SIMPLE STEPS

1. Under ABILITIES & TALENTS, list activities and fields you're naturally good at or that you've learned to do well: *athletics, writing, singing, art, teaching, management, sales, engineering.*

2. Under INTERESTS & PASSIONS, list activities and subjects that draw your attention and excite you: *investing, gardening, sailing, music, politics, metaphysics, business, animal rights.*

3. Review the above two lists and the PLEASANT WAYS TO GET MY MONEY list (Chapter 6). Cross off items as you choose to. For instance, you may be good at sales but prefer not to sell.

4. Review the above three lists and, under OCCUPATION, list potential callings. Look carefully at any items that appear on more than one of the three lists. Try combining some of the items: *singing teacher, metaphysics writer, business manager.*

5. Review your OCCUPATION list. Put stars next to items, cross off items, mix and match items, and add items as you see fit.

6. You may or may not find your "life's work" right now. Perhaps you'll at least find a worthwhile way to earn some money for a time. Unless inspired to act, wait for guidance. If you decide on a new field, working in it can become a step in one of your money-goal plans and a subgoal needing its own plan of action.

WHAT OTHERS HAVE WRITTEN

… find your unique talent, serve humanity with it,
and you can generate all the wealth that you want.
—Deepak Chopra, *The Seven
Spiritual Laws of Success*,
1994

If you want to be successful,
select a vocation you love.
—Thomas J. Stanley, *The Millionaire Mind*, 2000

Right livelihood has within itself its own rewards; it
deepens the person who practices it.
—Michael Phillips, *The Seven Laws of Money*,
1974

Do work you love where you keep expanding
your natural talents and passions and
adapt *those* to the marketplace.
—Cheryl Gilman, *Doing Work You Love*,
1997

Powerful people know how to find their niche.
They follow their passion.
—Nancy Anderson, *Work with Passion*, 1984

Do the things that you like doing.
Make them your job.
—Richard Koch, *The 80/20 Principle*, 1998

What you'll be happiest doing is built into your
nature like flying is built into a bird's.
—Barbara Sher with Barbara Smith,
Live the Life You Love, 1996

18

SELF-IMAGE

Your present situation, be it one of prosperity or poverty, of sickness or health, of self-confidence and social acceptance, or frustration and failure, is an exact reflection of your self-image.

—John K. Williams
The Wisdom of Your Subconscious Mind, 1964

CONCEPTS AND COUNSEL

Your *self-image* is made up of your conscious and subconscious beliefs about yourself. It governs what you do, have, and what happens to you. To create and maintain your ideal finances, you need the self-image of a person capable and deserving of doing so.

Your self-image should not depend on possessions, position, money, or social standing. It should not depend on anything outside you, though it can include such factors.

Your self-image should rest on a strong spiritual foundation. To help build that foundation, seek spiritual truth, look deeply inward, be open to your higher self, and be open to the Higher Power.

To prepare to create your new self-image, first find out, to the extent you can, what you believe about yourself now. Next, see and accept yourself as you truly are. Finally, decide how you want to be.

Then create your new self-image: visualize and imagine yourself looking, acting, performing, and living like the person you want to be; use affirmations to program in the traits and abilities you want to have; and think as if, feel as if, speak as if, and act as if you are the person you are striving to become.

In time, you will convince your subconscious mind that you are that person. Then your spontaneous thoughts, feelings, words, actions, and circumstances will show you *are* that person.

Always remember that who you are and where you are stem from your inner image of who you are and where you belong. You can become someone else. You can get somewhere else. You can change the outer image. First, though, you must change the inner image—your self-image.

SIMPLE STEPS

1. Stand before a mirror. Ponder your conscious beliefs about yourself. Think about what your environment and behavior reveal about your conscious and subconscious beliefs about yourself.

2. Under My Present Self-Image, list the beliefs about yourself you now know of: *worthy/unworthy*; *good with money/not good with money*; *outgoing/shy*; *industrious/lazy*; *fat/thin*; *smart/stupid*.

3. Read the list over. Mark each item with an *F* for *fact* (fat) or an *O* for *opinion* (stupid). Love and accept yourself regardless of the negative facts. Begin to release your negative opinions.

4. Under The New Me, list those abilities and traits you'd like to take on or improve upon: *good health*; *good with money*; *good with people*; *outgoing*; *confident*; *capable*; *wise*; *energetic*.

5. Refer to your The New Me list for ideas and write some affirmations under Self-Image Affirmations: *I am healthy*; *I am good with money*; *I am outgoing*; *I am confident*; *I am wise*; *I deserve and attract wealth*. Do these affirmations daily.

6. Review your The New Me and Self-Image Affirmations lists. Close your eyes, relax, and see yourself as you want to be. Each day, develop and dwell on these images and use your self-image affirmations as you visualize and imagine your new self.

WHAT OTHERS HAVE WRITTEN

The 'self-image' sets the boundaries
of individual accomplishment.
—Maxwell Maltz, M.D., *Psycho Cybernetics*, 1960

Your self-image is the most dominant factor
that affects everything you attempt to do.
—Dr. Walter Doyle Staples, *Think Like a Winner*,
1991

Successful people realize that their self-image
governs their success and work
to *reshape* that image.
—Sam Silverstein, *The Success Model*,
1993

Winners dwell on and hold the self-image of
that person they would most like to become.
—Dr. Denis Waitley, *The Psychology of Winning*,
1979

No one can ever go beyond
the self-image ... he holds.
—Bruce I. Doyle III, *Before You Think
Another Thought*,
1994

We cannot manifest anything that is
contrary to the image of self in our mind.
—Lucius Humphrey, *It Shall Be Done Unto You*, 1936

The starting point for both success and
happiness is a healthy self-image.
—Zig Ziglar, *See You at the Top*, 1975

19

PERSONAL ENERGY

The challenge of great performance is to manage your energy more effectively in all dimensions to achieve your goals.

—Jim Loehr and Tony Schwartz
The Power of Full Engagement, 2003

CONCEPTS AND COUNSEL

Your *personal energy* is your capacity for mental and physical activity. If you manage your energy effectively, you'll be better able to do what you need to do to get all the money you want to get.

Personal energy flows in the direction of thought, emotion, attention, intention, and action. By expressing your energy through these avenues, you cause yourself to either attract or repel money.

Your energy will flow best when its path is unobstructed. Poor physical health presents a major obstacle to the movement of energy through your body—a sick body restricts the flow of energy like a clogged water pipe restricts the flow of water.

There are many ways to regain and maintain your health and energy: eat a wholesome diet; drink enough pure water; breathe fully and get plenty of fresh air; get sufficient sleep, rest, relaxation, recreation, exercise, sunshine, and natural light; limit your intake of, and exposure to, harmful and poisonous substances and influences; avoid stress, negative emotions, and sexual excess; and smile, laugh, and be happy.

Each day, you wake up recharged with only so much new energy. When you use it up, you'll need to sleep again to get more. Spend your energy on matters of real importance to you.

Take periodic breaks from your labor (minutes, hours, days, weeks). Without adequate rest and time away from your mental and physical work, your ability to do that work effectively will decline.

Personal energy makes human life possible. Personal energy used well will give rise to a life lived well. A life lived well will bring prosperity to the one who lives it and, as a result, to countless others.

SIMPLE STEPS

1. Learn how to get and stay healthy. Here are some subjects you may want to look into: the vegetarian, vegan, raw food, and fruitarian diets; fasting; exercise; sunshine and natural light; Shivambu; water drinking; holistic dentistry; and alternative medicine.

2. Improve your diet. You may not fully adopt any of the above ways of eating, but you will gain helpful insight by learning about them. To get you started, here's some general food advice for you to consider: choose whole over processed; choose plant over animal; choose organic over commercially grown; choose raw over cooked; and choose less over more. And eat slower. And chew well.

3. Develop healthful habits: walk, use the stairs, ride a bike; open some windows and curtains; go to sleep early and wake up early; spend time outside; spend time alone; don't hurry or worry; maintain a positive mental attitude; find peace of mind; and so on.

4. Each day, while exercising and whenever else you choose to, affirm, *I am healthy, strong, fit, and full of energy.* Come up with some affirmations to address your specific health needs.

5. Visualize and imagine your ideal physical condition. To add power and focus, do your health affirmations at the same time.

6. When you don't seem to have the energy you need, act as if you do. Or, if you can, rest or sleep.

WHAT OTHERS HAVE WRITTEN

Helping yourself to riches entails the output of an
enormous amount of energy. Good health is therefore
an essential part of becoming successful.
—Brian Adams, *Grow Rich with Your
Million Dollar Mind*, 1991

Eliminate from your life diffusive
expenditure of energy.
—Frank Channing Haddock, *The Secret
of Brain Energy*, 1910

To consume our vital essence in the sexual act
weakens body and brain, dulls the senses, and
deteriorates the body. To refrain from the act ...
conserves the vital essence, sharpens the
senses, and invigorates the body.
—Hilton Hotema, *Awaken the World Within*, 1962

The most overlooked area of health is exercise.
—Brian R. Clement, *Exercise:
Creating Your Persona*, 1994

... energy must be replaced by sleep
and by sleep alone.
—Hereward Carrington, *Vitality, Fasting and Nutrition*,
1908

The shortest and safest path to health is fasting.
—Arnold Ehret, *Kranke Menschen*, 1910

The body needs very little food, much
less than people realize.
—Paul Nison, *The Raw Life*, 2000

20

RADIATE
FINANCIAL INCREASE

Increase is what all men and all women are seeking; it is the urge of the Formless Intelligence within them, seeking fuller expression.

—Wallace D. Wattles
The Science of Getting Rich, 1910

CONCEPTS AND COUNSEL

To *radiate financial increase*, you express the energy of prosperity with an emphasis on monetary gain. This energy goes out and helps others get the money they want and need. Then this energy returns to help *you* get the money *you* want and need.

Your main thought in radiating financial increase should be to help *others* get money. *Your* return will come as a result of doing that. An easy way to help people get money is to always speak to them of gain and plenty and never of loss or lack.

A far-reaching—and at the same time private—way to help people get more money is to think about, imagine, and visualize monetary gain and abundance for specific people and for all people throughout the world.

A straightforward way to help people get money is to simply *give it* to them. For instance, you could hand money to homeless people, tip service people more than they expect, or give money to someone you know has a pressing need for it. Though people grow by learning to meet their financial needs and desires, wise giving can often help both giver and receiver.

The *best* way, and a *permanent* way, to help people get more money is to teach them how they can attract it by using their minds properly. So, when you feel a certain person might be open to hearing about it, you can share some of what you have learned about the subject. If you like, you can recommend or give good books on the subject.

You can radiate financial increase with your thoughts, words, and deeds. What you do for others, you do for yourself. Help people get more money, and you help yourself to do the same.

SIMPLE STEPS

1. Review your WHY I WANT MORE MONEY and MY NEW LIFE lists (Chapters 1 and 5). Know that all people want increase and improvement just as you do, and that having more money can either directly or indirectly help them get most of what they want.

2. Under CAN I HELP YOU?, list some people you know, or know of, who have a pressing need for money. If you think any of those people would be open to receiving it, consider giving them a gift of money. Give it anonymously if you choose to.

3. Under SHARE THE KNOWLEDGE, list the people you know who know about, or who you think might at least be open to hearing about, the techniques for using mind power to attract money.

4. Next to each name on the list, write an R for recommend or a G for give. As the opportunities present themselves, recommend this book and/or give copies of it to those on your list.

5. If you feel it would be right for you, form a small group to study and discuss this book. As the group sees fit, study and discuss other pertinent books as well. Meet weekly, biweekly, or monthly. Select a group leader, or teacher, as appropriate.

6. On a 3"x5" index card, write RADIATE FINANCIAL IN-CREASE. Put the card where you will see it at least two or three times daily.

WHAT OTHERS HAVE WRITTEN

What you radiate determines what
your manifest world will be.
—E.V. Ingraham, *Wells of Abundance*, 1938

Giving and receiving is one in truth.
—Wally "Famous" Amos and Gregory Amos,
The Power in You, 1988

The more you include in all your striving a desire
for the good of others along with your own
welfare, the more you will thrive.
—J. Donald Walters, *Money Magnetism*,
1992

The more you help others, the more you
attract that same energy to you.
—James Arthur Ray, *The Science of Success*, 2006

Every thought you express and every condition
you create in the lives of others will
return to you in the same spirit.
—R. C. Allen, *The Secret of Success*,
1965

You will profit best by helping others succeed.
—Walter M. Germain, *The Magic Power of Your Mind*,
1956

No one can become rich in any way without
enriching others. Anyone who adds to
prosperity must prosper in turn.
—Earl Nightingale, *This Is Earl Nightingale*,
1969

AFTERWORD

Thank you for reading this book. I hope you have enjoyed it. And I hope you will continue to benefit from having read it. I have benefited greatly from having read countless books over the years.

I began to find my first self-help, spiritual, and metaphysical books in my early twenties, not long after I moved from New Jersey to California to try to find my way in the world. Before that move, I had no idea such books even existed.

And honestly, were it not for such books and my intense desire to learn, to grow, and to improve myself and my circumstances, I would have gone down a completely different road in life—a road I would rather not even think about or imagine.

Who could deny the assertion that books can and do change lives? It is my mission to write some of those books that do indeed change lives. I want people's lives to be better because I lived and because I wrote.

There are reasons I came into this life, and writing is one of them. I am living the life I was meant to live, and it is my sincere desire that you will live the life you were meant to live.

Can I ask two favors of you?

First, if you think this or any of my other books can help people in some of the ways they could use help, will you help spread the word about me and my writings? You could do that by loaning my books to others, giving my books as gifts, and by telling people about my books and about me. By doing these things, you will bless me beyond measure, and I truly believe you will bless others beyond measure as well.

Second, please consider writing an honest review for this book. Reviews are important to the success of any book and any author. And reviews really do help people decide whether or not a certain book is right for them. So, by writing a review, you will be helping me personally and other people as well.

And speaking of those other people: Say your review is the one that causes a person to actually buy this or any of my other books. And suppose that person then reads the book. And suppose that book helps that person to substantially improve their own life and the lives of others. Just imagine the possibilities—lives made better because you wrote a book review.

Currently, Amazon.com is the most important place you could post a review, but feel free to post a review anywhere you choose. And keep in mind, even just a sentence or two could be sufficient. The number of words in a review you write is less important than what those words say.

If you do write reviews for any of my books, feel free to let me know by contacting me on one of my social-media pages, by email, or however else you can. I will enjoy hearing from you and reading your review.

Finally, always remember, you are capable of so much more than you have ever imagined. Learn, believe, act, and persist. Do those four things, and nothing will stop you from continuing to build a better and better life for yourself and for those you care about.

Peace & Plenty . . .

ABOUT THE AUTHOR

James Goi Jr., aka The Attract Money Guru™, is the bestselling author of the internationally published *How to Attract Money Using Mind Power*, a book that set a new standard for concise, no-nonsense, straight-to-the-point self-help books. First published in 2007, that game-changing book continues to transform lives around the world. And though it would be years before James would write new books, and even more years before he would publish new books, that first book set the tone for his writing career. The tagline for James as an author and publisher is Books to Awaken, Uplift, and Empower™. And James takes those words seriously, as is evident in every book he writes. James: is a relative recluse and spends most of his time alone; is an advanced mind-power practitioner, a natural-born astral traveler, and an experienced lucid dreamer; has had life-changing encounters with both angels and demons and even sees some dead people; has been the grateful recipient of an inordinate amount of life-saving divine intervention; is a poet and songwriter; is a genuinely nice guy who cares about people and all forms of life; fasts regularly; is a sincere seeker of higher human health; is an objective observer, a persistent ponderer, and a deliberate deducer; and has a supple sense of heady humor.

STAY IN TOUCH WITH JAMES

If you are a sincere seeker of spiritual truth and/or a determined pursuer of material wealth and success, James could be the lifeline and the go-to resource you have been hoping to find. Step One, subscribe to James's free monthly *Mind Power & Money Ezine* here: jamesgoijr.com/subscriber-page.html. Step Two, connect with James online anywhere and everywhere you can find him. You can start here:

Facebook.com/JamesGoiJr
Facebook.com/JamesGoiJrPublicPage
Facbook.com/HowToAttractMoneyUsingMindPower
Twitter.com/JamesGoiJr
Linkedin.com/in/JamesGoiJr
Pinterest.com/JamesGoiJr
Plus.Google.com/+JamesGoiJr
Youtube.com/JamesGoiJr
Instagram.com/JamesGoiJr
Goodreads.com/JamesGoiJr
jamesgoijr.tumblr.com

James's Amazon Author Page

A great resource to help you keep abreast of James's ever-expanding list of books is his Author Central page at Amazon.com. There you will find all of his published writings and have easy access to them in the various editions in which they will be published. Here is where you can go to check out James's page on Amazon:

amazon.com/author/JamesGoiJr

SPECIAL ACKNOWLEDGEMENT

To Kathy Darlene Hunt, who has been my rock, my Light, my safety net, and my buffer since I was in my twenties. She rightfully shares in the credit for every book I've written, for the books I'm working on now, and for every single book I will ever write.

A FREE GIFT FOR YOU!

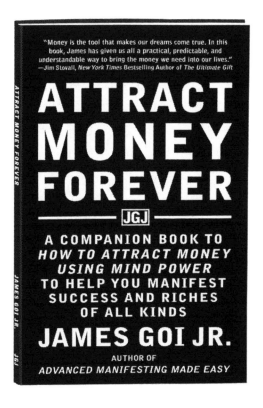

Attract Money Forever will deepen your understanding of metaphysics and mind-power principles as they relate to attracting money, manifesting abundance, and governing material reality. You'll learn how to use time-tested, time-honored, practical, and spiritual techniques to be more prosperous and improve your life in astounding and meaningful ways. Visit jamesgoijr.com/subscriber-page.html for your free download copy of this amazing book and to receive James's free monthly *Mind Power & Money Ezine*.

BIBLIOGRAPHY

NOTE: The dates used in the chapters of this book are the original copyright or publication dates. The dates used in this bibliography are the latest copyright or publication dates given in the editions consulted. Also, in the chapters of this book, many of the subtitles were left out; all subtitles are listed in this bibliography. Some book titles have changed. Some books have been republished with other books under one title, and so on. The titles listed in the chapters are the original titles, and the titles listed in this bibliography are the titles of the editions consulted. The author will appreciate any feedback on errors or omissions in this bibliography.

Adams, Brian. *Grow Rich with Your Million Dollar Mind*. North Hollywood, CA: Wilshire Book Company, 1991.

Addington, Jack and Cornelia Addington. *Your Needs Met*. San Diego, CA: Abundant Living Foundation, 1978.

Alexander, Scott. *Rhinoceros Success*. Laguna Hills, CA: The Rhino's Press, 1980.

Allen, James. *As a Man Thinketh*. New York: G.P. Putnam's Sons, No date.

Allen, Marc. *The Millionaire Course: A Visionary Plan for Creating the Life of Your Dreams*. Novato, CA: New World Library, 2003.

Allen, R. C. *The Secret of Success*. Louisville, KY: Best Books, Inc., 1965.

Amos, Wally and Gregory Amos. *The Power in You: Ten Secret Ingredients for Inner Strength*. New York: Donald I. Fine, Inc., 1988.

Andersen, U. S. *The Magic in Your Mind*. North Hollywood, CA: Wilshire Book Company, 1961.

Anderson, Brenda. *Playing the Quantum Field: How Changing Your Choices Can Change Your Life*. Novato, CA: New World Library, 2006.

Anderson, Nancy. *Work with Passion: How to Do What You Love for a Living*. San Rafael, CA: Whatever Publishing, Inc., 1992.

Anthony, Robert. *Dr. Robert Anthony's Advanced Formula for Total Success*. New York: Berkley Books, 1988.

Atkinson, William Walker. *Dynamic Thought, or The Law of Vibrant Energy.* Los Angeles: The Segnogram Publishing Company, 1906. (Reprinted 1976 by Health Research, Pomeroy, WA.)

Aurelius, Marcus. *Meditations.* Mineola, NY: Dover Publications, Inc., 1977.

Barker, Raymond Charles. *The Science of Successful Living.* Marina del Rey, CA: DeVorss & Company, 1985.

Behrend, Genevieve. *Your Invisible Power.* N.P.: N.pub., 1927. (Reprinted by Health Research, Pomeroy, WA.)

Besant, Annie. *Thought Power, Its Control and Culture.* Wheaton, IL: The Theosophical Publishing House, 1984.

Bloodworth, Venice J. *Key to Yourself.* Marina del Rey, CA: Devorss & Company, 1980.

Brande, Dorothea. *Wake up and Live!* New York: Cornerstone Library, 1936.

Bristol, Claude M. *The Magic of Believing.* New York: Simon & Schuster, 1985.

Brown, Henry Harrison. *How to Control Fate through Suggestion.* N.P.: N.pub., 1906. (Reprinted 1972 by Health Research, Pomeroy, WA.)

Brown, Les. *Live Your Dreams.* New York: Avon Books, 1992.

Brownell, Louise B. *Life Abundant for You.* Santa Barbara, CA: The Aquarian Ministry, 1933.

Bry, Adelaide with Marjorie Bair. *Visualization: Directing the Movies of Your Mind.* New York: Barnes & Noble Books, 1979.

Butler-Bowden, Tom. *50 Success Classics: Winning Wisdom for Work and Life from 50 Landmark Books*. Boston: Nicholas Brealey Publishing, 2004.

Butterworth, Eric. *Spiritual Economics: The Prosperity Process*. Unity Village, MO: Unity School of Christianity, 1984.

Byrne, Rhonda. *The Secret*. New York: Atria Books and Beyond Words Publishing, Hillsboro, OR, 2006.

Cady, H. Emilie. *Lessons in Truth*. Unity Village, MO: Unity Books, 1895.

Canfield, Jack and Mark Victor Hansen. *Dare to Win*. New York: Berkley Books, 1996.

Carlson, Richard. *Don't Worry, Make Money: Spiritual and Practical Ways to Create Abundance and More Fun in Your Life*. New York: Hyperion, 1997.

Carrington, Hereward. *Vitality, Fasting and Nutrition*. New York: Rebman Company, No date. (Reprinted by Health Research, Pomeroy, WA.)

Carroll, Lenedra J. *The Architecture of All Abundance: Creating a Successful Life in the Material World*. Novato, CA: New World Library, 2001.

Chopra, Deepak. *The Seven Spiritual Laws of Success: A Practical Guide to the Fulfillment of Your Dreams*. San Rafael, CA: Amber-Allen Publishing and New World Library, 1994.

Clayson, George S. *The Richest Man in Babylon*. New York: Plume, 1955.

Clement, Brian R. *Exercise: Creating Your Persona*. West Palm Beach, FL: A.M. Press, 1994.

Collier, Robert. *The Secret of the Ages*. Indialantic, FL: Robert Collier Publications, Inc., 1995.

Curtis, Donald. *Science of Mind in Daily Living*. North Hollywood, CA: Wilshire Book Company, 1975.

Day, Laura. *Practical Intuition: How to Harness the Power of Your Instinct and Make It Work for You.* New York: Villard Books, 1996.

De Laurence, L. W. *The Master Key.* Chicago: The de Laurence Company, 1914. (Reprinted by Health Research, Pomeroy, WA.)

Demartini, John F. *Count Your Blessings: The Healing Power of Gratitude and Love.* Carlsbad, CA: Hay House, Inc., 2006.

Devoe, Walter. *Mystic Words of Mighty Power.* Chicago: College of Freedon, 1905. (Reprinted 1971 by Health Research, Pomeroy, WA.)

Douglas, Mack R. *Making a Habit of Success.* New York: Galahad Books, 1999.

Doyle, Bob. *Wealth Beyond Reason: Your Complete Handbook for Boundless Living.* Victoria, B.C., Canada: Trafford Publishing and Boundless Living Publishing, 2003.

Doyle, Bruce I. *Before You Think Another Thought: An Illustrated Guide to Understanding How Your Thoughts and Beliefs Create Your Life.* Charlottesville, VA: Hampton Roads Publishing Company, 1997.

Drury, Ruth. *Tapping into Prosperity: The Universal Path to Success.* N.P.: Prosperity Times Publishing Company, 1991.

Dyer, Wayne W. *Real Magic: Creating Miracles in Everyday Life.* New York: HarperCollinsPublishers, 1992.

Edwards, William E. *Ten Days to a Great New Life.* North Hollywood, CA: Wilshire Book Company, 1963.

Ehret, Arnold. *The Cause and Cure of Human Illness.* Dobbs Ferry, NY: The Ehret Literature Publishing Company, Inc., 2001.

Eker, T. Harv. *Secrets of the Millionaire Mind: Mastering the Inner Game of Wealth.* New York: HarperBusiness, 2005.

Elgin, Duane. *Voluntary Simplicity: Toward a Way of Life That Is Outwardly Simple, Inwardly Rich.* New York: William Morrow and Company, Inc., 1981.

Emerson, Ralph Waldo. *Selected Writings of Ralph Waldo Emerson.* New York: New American Library, 1965.

Fillmore, Charles. *Prosperity.* Unity Village, MO: Unity House, 2005.

Forster, Sandy. *How to Be Wildly Wealthy Fast: A Powerful Step by Step Guide to Attract Prosperity and Abundance into Your Life Today.* Mooloolaba, Qld, Australia: Universal Prosperity Pty Ltd, 2005.

Fox, Emmet. *Power through Constructive Thinking.* New York: Harper & Brothers Publishers, 1940.

Franklin, Benjamin. *Autobiography.* Boston: Bedford Books of St. Martin's Press, 1993.

Gains, Edwene. *The Four Spiritual Laws of Prosperity: A Simple Guide to Unlimited Abundance.* N.P.: Rodale, Inc., 2005.

Gawain, Shakti. *Creative Visualization.* Mill Valley, CA: Whatever Publishing, Inc., 1982.

Germain, Walter M. *The Magic Power of Your Mind: How to Unleash Your Hidden Powers*. North Hollywood, CA: Wilshire Book Company, 1956.

Gilman, Cheryl. *Doing Work You Love: Discovering Your Purpose and Realizing Your Dreams*. New York: Barnes & Noble Books, Inc., 1997.

Goldsmith, Joel S. *Invisible Supply: Finding the Gifts of the Spirit Within*. San Francisco: HarperSanFrancisco, 1994.

Gracian, Baltasar. *The Art of Worldly Wisdom: A Pocket Oracle*. New York: Doubleday, 1992.

Graham, Stedman. *You Can Make It Happen: A Nine-Step Plan for Success*. New York: Simon & Schuster, 1997.

Grayson, Stuart. *The Ten Demandments of Prosperity*. New York: Dodd, Mead & Company, 1986.

Gregory, Eva. *The Feel Good Guide to Prosperity*. San Francisco: Leading Edge Publishers, 2004.

Haanel, Charles F. *The Master Key System*. Wilkes-Barre, PA: Kallisti Publishing, 2000.

Haddock, Frank Channing. *The Secret of Brain Energy: Scientific Methods in Using Your Powers for Personal and Financial Success*. Meriden, CT: The Pelton Publishing Company, 1923. (Reprinted 1988 by Health Research, Pomeroy, WA.)

Hamblin, Henry Thomas. *Dynamic Thought*. N.P.: Yogi Publication Society, 1923.

Harris, Herbert. *The Twelve Universal Laws of Success*. Wilmington, NC: The LifeSkill® Institute, Inc., 2005.

Hay, Louise L. *The Power Is Within You*. Carlsbad, CA: Hay House, Inc., 2005.

Hiatt, Marta. *Mind Magic: Techniques for Transforming Your Life.* St. Paul, MN: Llewellyn Publications, 2005.

Hicks, Esther and Jerry Hicks. *The Law of Attraction: The Basics of the Teachings of Abraham.* Carlsbad, CA: Hay House, Inc., 2006.

Hill, Napoleon. *Think and Grow Rich.* New York: Fawcett Crest, 1960.

Holliwell, Raymond. *Working with the Law.* Camarillo, CA: Devorss Publications, 2006.

Holmes, Ernest. *The Science of Mind.* New York: Dodd, Mead and Company, 1938.

Hopkins, Tom. *The Official Guide to Success.* New York: Warner Books, Inc., 1984.

Hotema, Hilton. *Awaken the World Within.* Mokelumne Hill, CA: Health Research, 1962.

Humphrey, Lucius. *It Shall Be Done unto You.* New York: Richard R. Smith, 1939.

Hunter, Roy. *Success through Mind Power: How to Be a Winner in the Game of Life.* Glendale, CA: Westwood Publishing Company, Inc., 1986.

Hutson, Don and Chris Crouch and George Lucas. *The Contented Achiever: How to Get What You Want and Love What You Get.* Memphis, TN: Black Pants Publishing, LLC, 2001.

Ingraham, E. V. *Wells of Abundance.* Marina del Rey, CA: Devorss & Company, 1966.

James, William. *The Will to Believe: The Works of William James.* Cambridge, MA: Harvard University Press, 1979.

John-Roger and Peter McWilliams. *Life 101: Everything We Wish We Had Learned About Life in School— But Didn't.* Los Angeles: Prelude Press, Inc., 1991.

Koch, Richard. *The 80/20 Principle: The Secret of Achieving More with Less.* New York: Doubleday, 1998.

Larson, C. D. *Mastery of Fate.* Cincinnati, OH: Eternal Progress, 1907. (Reprinted by Health Research, Pomeroy, WA.)

Loehr, Jim and Tony Schwartz. *The Power of Full Engagement: Managing Energy, Not Time, Is the Key to High Performance and Personal Renewal.* New York: Free Press, 2003.

Lorayne, Harry. *Secrets of Mind Power.* New York: Frederick Fell, Inc., 1961.

Lunde, Norman S. *You Unlimited.* Marina del Rey, CA: Devorss and Company, 1988.

MacDougall, Mary Katherine. *Prosperity Now.* Lee's Summit, MO: Unity Books, 1969.

Mackenzie, Alec. *Time for Success: A Goal Getter's Strategy.* New York: McGraw-Hill Publishing Company, 1989.

Maltz, Maxwell. *Psycho Cybernetics: A New Way to Get More Living Out of Life.* North Hollywood, CA: Wilshire Book Company, 1960.

Mandino, Og. *The Greatest Success in the World.* New York: Bantam Books, 1982.

Marden, Orison Swett. *How to Get What You Want.* New York: Thomas Y. Crowell Company, 1917.

McCollum, Harriet Luella. *What Makes a Master?* N.P.: N.pub., 1932. (Reprinted 1975 by Health Research, Pomeroy, WA.)

McMonagle, Gary R. *Instant Money: How to Use the Hidden Power of Your Mind to Attract Incredible Wealth.* Warren, OH: RMA Publishing, 1991.

Militz, Annie Rix. *Both Riches and Honor.* Lee's Summit, MO: Unity Books, 1945.

Milteer, Lee. *Success Is an Inside Job: Heart, Integrity, and Intuition—the Secrets to Getting Anything You Want.* Charlottesville, VA: Hampton Roads Publishing Company, Inc., 1996.

Mohr, Barbel. *The Cosmic Ordering Service.* Charlottesville, VA: Hampton Roads Publishing Company, Inc., 2001.

Mulford, Prentice. *Thoughts Are Things.* N.P.: N.pub., No date. (Reprinted by Health Research, Pomeroy, WA.)

Murphy, Joseph. *The Power of Your Subconscious Mind.* Englewood Cliffs, NJ: Prentice-Hall, Inc., 1978.

Newberry, Tommy. *Success Is Not an Accident: Change Your Choices, Change Your Life.* Decatur, GA: Looking Glass Books, 2000.

Nightingale, Earl. *This Is Earl Nightingale.* Chicago: Nightingale-Conant Corporation, 1983.

Nison, Paul. *The Raw Life: Becoming Natural in an Unnatural World.* New York: 343 Publishing Company, 2001.

Norman, Ernest L. *The Infinite Concept of Cosmic Creation.* El Cajon, CA: Unarius Academy of Science, 1998.

Norris, Chuck with Joe Hyams. *The Secret of Inner Strength: My Story*. Boston: Little, Brown and Company, 1988.

Odle, Chris. *Practical Visualization: Self-Development through Visualization and Affirmation*. Wellingborough, Northamptonshire, England: The Aquarian Press, 1990.

Olson, Dale W. *Knowing Your Intuitive Mind*. Eugene, OR: Crystalline Publications, 1994.

Orman, Suze. *The Courage to Be Rich: Creating a Life of Material and Spiritual Abundance*. New York: Riverhead Books, 1999.

Peale, Norman Vincent. *The Power of Positive Thinking*. New York: Prentice-Hall, Inc., 1954.

Phillips, Michael. *The Seven Laws of Money*. Boston: Shambhala Publications, Inc., 1997.

Ponder, Catherine. *The Dynamic Laws of Prosperity*. Marina del Rey, CA: Devorss Publications, 1985.

Powers, Melvin. *Dynamic Thinking: The Technique for Achieving Self-Confidence and Success*. North Hollywood, CA: Wilshire Book Company, 1955.

Price, John Randolph. *The Abundance Book*. Carlsbad, CA: Hay House, Inc., 2005.

Proctor, Bob. *You Were Born Rich*. Cartersville, GA: LifeSuccess Productions, 1997.

Ray, James Arthur. *The Science of Success: How to Attract Prosperity and Create Harmonic Wealth through Proven Principles*. Carlsbad, CA: SunArk Press, 2006.

Rellimeo. *Within the Holy of Holies, or Attitudes of Attainment.* Chicago: The Mastery Publishing Company, 1920. (Reprinted 1974 by Health Research, Pomeroy, WA.)

Robbins, Anthony. *Unlimited Power.* New York: Ballantine Books, 1987.

Robinson, Lynn A. *Real Prosperity: Using the Power of Intuition to Create Financial and Spiritual Abundance.* Kansas City, MO: Andrews McMeel Publishing, 2004.

Roman, Sanaya and Duane Packer. *Creating Money: Keys to Abundance.* Tiburon, CA: H.J. Kramer, Inc., 1988.

Rosenthal, Allen. *Your Mind the Magician.* Marina del Rey, CA: Devorss Publications, 1991.

Russell, Robert A. *You Too Can Be Prosperous: Studies in Prosperity.* Camarillo, CA: Devorss Publications, 1950.

Schwartz, David J. *The Magic of Thinking Big.* Englewood Cliffs, NJ: Prentice-Hall, Inc., 1960.

Seale, Ervin. *Ten Words That Will Change Your Life.* Los Angeles: Science of Mind Publications, 1979.

Seton, Julia. *The Science of Success.* New York: Edward J. Clode, 1914. (Reprinted 1972 by Health Research, Pomeroy, WA.)

Shanklin, Imelda Octavia. *What Are You?* Unity Village, MO: Unity Books, 1995.

Sher, Barbara with Barbara Smith. *Live the Life You Love: In Ten Easy Step-by-Step Lessons.* New York: Dell Publishing, 1997.

Sherman, Harold. *The New TNT, Miraculous Power Within You.* Englewood Cliffs, NJ: Prentice-Hall, Inc., 1967.

Shinn, Florence Scovel. *The Game of Life and How to Play It.* New York: Fireside, 1986.

Silverstein, Sam. *The Success Model: The Five Step System to Completely Revolutionize Your Life.* St. Louis, MO: Star Publishing, 1993.

Simmons, Charles M. *Your Subconscious Power: How to Make it Work for You.* North Hollywood, CA: Wilshire Book Company, 1965.

Sinetar, Marsha. *Do What You Love, the Money Will Follow: Discovering Your Right Livelihood.* New York: Dell Publishing, 1989.

Smiles, Samuel. *Thrift, or How to Get On in the World.* Chicago: Belford, Clarke & Company, 1885.

Stallone, Sylvester. *Sly Moves: My Proven Program to Lose Weight, Build Strength, Gain Will Power, and Live Your Dream.* New York: HarperResource, 2005.

Stanley, Thomas J. *The Millionaire Mind.* Kansas City, MO: Andrews McMeel Publishing, 2000.

Staples, Walter Doyle. *Think Like a Winner.* North Hollywood, CA: Wilshire Book Company, 1991.

Stiles, Bill. *Mind Power to Success.* N.P.: N.pub., 1986.

Stone, W. Clement. *The Success System That Never Fails.* Wise, VA: The Napoleon Hill Foundation, 2004.

Stortz, Margaret R. *Start Living Every Day of Your Life: How to Use the Science of Mind.* Los Angeles: Science of Mind Publications, 1981.

Sweetland, Ben. *I Can: The Key to Life's Golden Secret*. North Hollywood, CA: Wilshire Book Company, 1953.

Taylor, Sandra Ann. *Quantum Success: The Astounding Science of Wealth and Happiness*. Carlsbad, CA: Hay House, Inc., 2006.

Templeton, John Marks. *Discovering the Laws of Life*. New York: The Continuum Publishing Company, 1994.

Thoreau, Henry David. *Walden, or Life in the Woods*. New York: Barnes & Noble Books, 1993.

Towne, Elizabeth. *How to Grow Success*. N.P.: N.pub., 1904. (Reprinted 1968 by Health Research, Pomeroy, WA.)

Towne, William E. *Health and Wealth from Within: How to Apply New Thought to the Attainment of Health, Success, and the Solving of Everyday Problems*. Holyoke, MA: Elizabeth Towne, 1909. (Republished 1968 by Health Research, Pomeroy, WA.)

Tracy, Brian. *Maximum Achievement: The Proven System of Strategies and Skills That Will Unlock Your Hidden Powers to Succeed*. New York: Simon & Schuster, 1993.

Trine, Ralph Waldo. *Character Building Thought Power*. New York: Thomas Y. Crowell & Company, 1900. (Reprinted 1976 by Health Research, Pomeroy, WA.)

Troward, Thomas. *The Hidden Power: And Other Papers upon Mental Science*. New York: Dodd, Mead & Company, 1947.

Van Fleet, James K. *Hidden Power: How to Unleash the Power of Your Subconscious Mind*. Paramus, NJ: Prentice-Hall, Inc., 1987.

Vanzant, Iyanla. *One Day My Soul Just Opened Up: 40 Days and 40 Nights Toward Spiritual Strength and Personal Growth*. New York: Fireside, 1998.

Vitale, Joe. *The Attractor Factor: 5 Easy Steps for Creating Wealth (or Anything Else) from the Inside Out*. Hoboken, NJ: John Wiley & Sons, Inc., 2005.

Waitley, Denis. *The Psychology of Winning*. New York: Berkley Books, 1984.

Walsch, Neale Donald. *Conversations with God: An Uncommon Dialog*. New York: G.P. Putnam's Sons, 1996.

Walters, J. Donald. *Money Magnetism: How to Attract What You Need When You Need It*. Nevada City, CA: Crystal Clarity Publishers, 1992.

Wattles, Wallace D. *Financial Success through Creative Thought, or The Science of Getting Rich*. Holyoke, MA: The Elizabeth Towne Company, Inc., 1927. (Reprinted by Health Research, Pomeroy, WA.)

West, Georgiana Tree. *Prosperity's Ten Commandments*. Unity Village, MO: Unity House, 2005.

Wilcox, Ella Wheeler. *Heart of the New Thought*. Chicago: The Psychic Research Company, 1902. (Reprinted 1971 by Health Research, Pomeroy, WA.)

Wilde, Stuart. *Affirmations*. Taos, NM: White Dove International, Inc., 1987.

Wilkinson, Winifred. *Miracle Power for Today*. Garden City, NY: Doubleday & Company, Inc., 1969.

Williams, John K. *The Wisdom of Your Subconscious Mind*. Englewood Cliffs, NJ: Prentice-Hall, Inc., 1973.

Wilmans, Helen. *The Conquest of Poverty.* Sea Breeze, FL: International Scientific Association, 1900. (Republished 1969 by Health Research, Pomeroy, WA.)

Yogananda, Paramahansa. *The Law of Success: Using the Power of Spirit to Create Health, Prosperity, and Happiness.* Los Angeles: Self-Realization Fellowship, 2002.

Ziglar, Zig. *See You at the Top.* Gretna, LA: Pelican Publishing Company, 1979.

Made in the USA
Middletown, DE
21 April 2018